# Ancient Rome for Kids

## Early History, Science, Architecture, Art and Government

### Ancient History for Kids
### 6th Grade Social Studies

**BABY PROFESSOR**
EDUCATION KIDS

Speedy Publishing LLC

40 E. Main St. #1156

Newark, DE 19711

www.speedypublishing.com

Copyright 2018

All Rights reserved. No part of this book may be reproduced or used in any way or form or by any means whether electronic or mechanical, this means that you cannot record or photocopy any material ideas or tips that are provided in this book.

In this book, we're going to talk about the city of Rome in ancient times. So, let's get right to it!

AERIAL VIEW OF THE CITY FROM ABOVE, ROME, ITALY

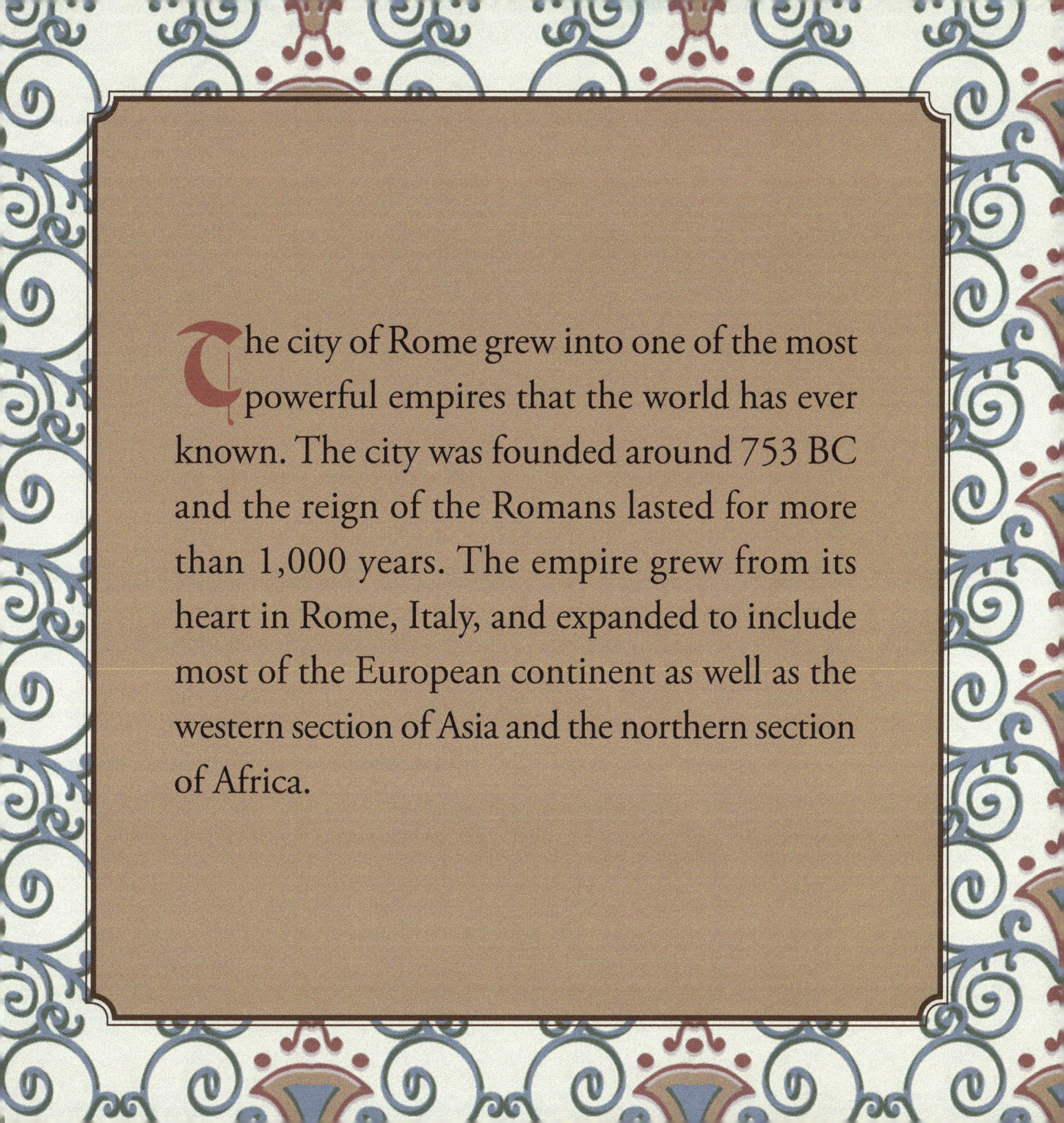

The city of Rome grew into one of the most powerful empires that the world has ever known. The city was founded around 753 BC and the reign of the Romans lasted for more than 1,000 years. The empire grew from its heart in Rome, Italy, and expanded to include most of the European continent as well as the western section of Asia and the northern section of Africa.

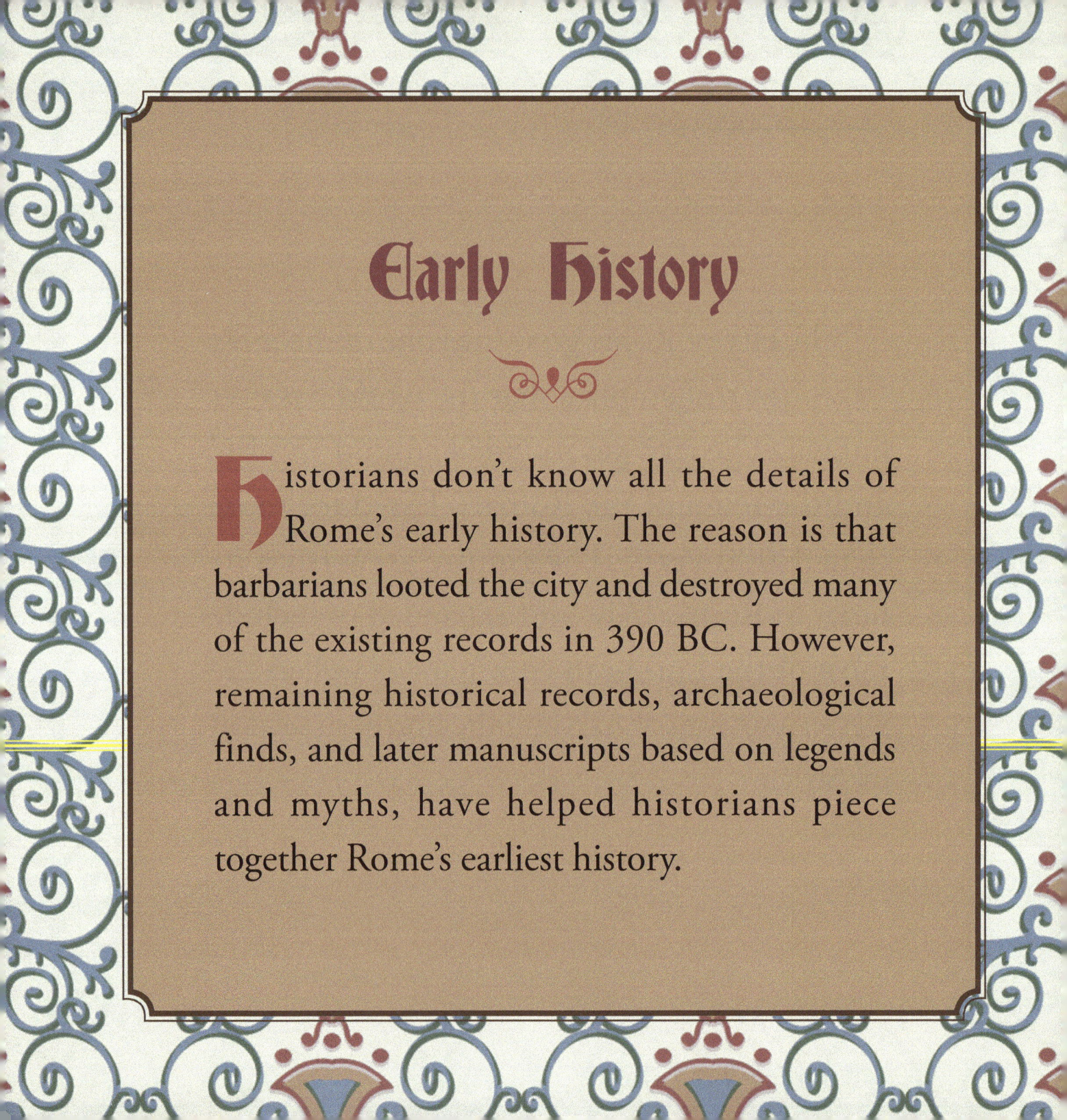

# Early History

Historians don't know all the details of Rome's early history. The reason is that barbarians looted the city and destroyed many of the existing records in 390 BC. However, remaining historical records, archaeological finds, and later manuscripts based on legends and myths, have helped historians piece together Rome's earliest history.

# BARBARIANS vs ROMANS

It's likely that the area we know today as Rome was first established as early as 1000 BC. Rome is known for its seven hills. The first hill that was populated was Palatine Hill.

## PALATINE HILL

This was a strategic choice because it was easy to keep secure since it stood 230 feet higher than most of the city's land.

Over a period of time, the other six hills in the area became populated and Rome expanded to become a big city. Between the Palatine hill and the Capitoline hill, a large public plaza was constructed, which eventually became known as Rome's Forum.

ROMAN FORUM AND PALATINE HILL

ROMULUS AND REMUS

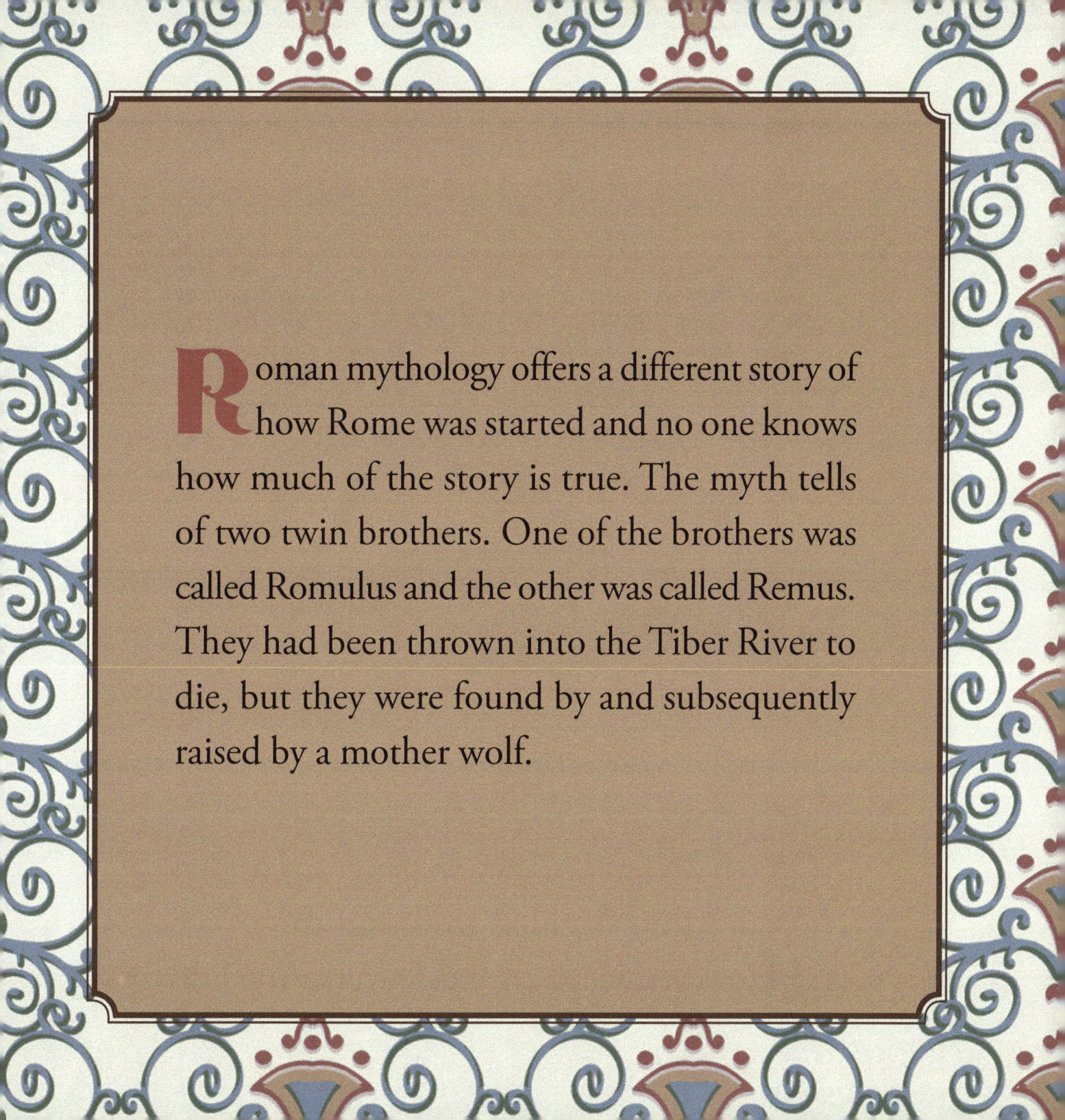

Roman mythology offers a different story of how Rome was started and no one knows how much of the story is true. The myth tells of two twin brothers. One of the brothers was called Romulus and the other was called Remus. They had been thrown into the Tiber River to die, but they were found by and subsequently raised by a mother wolf.

Iulio Romano inu:
W. Hollar fecit 1652
Ex Collectione J. Nicolai Lanieri

As they grew up, they were natural leaders and they decided to found their own city. However, when they discovered the hills

**A SHE-WOLF SUCKLING THE INFANTS ROMULUS AND REMUS**

of Rome, they fought over which hill should be the prime building site. The fighting became more intense.

# ROMAN FORUMS

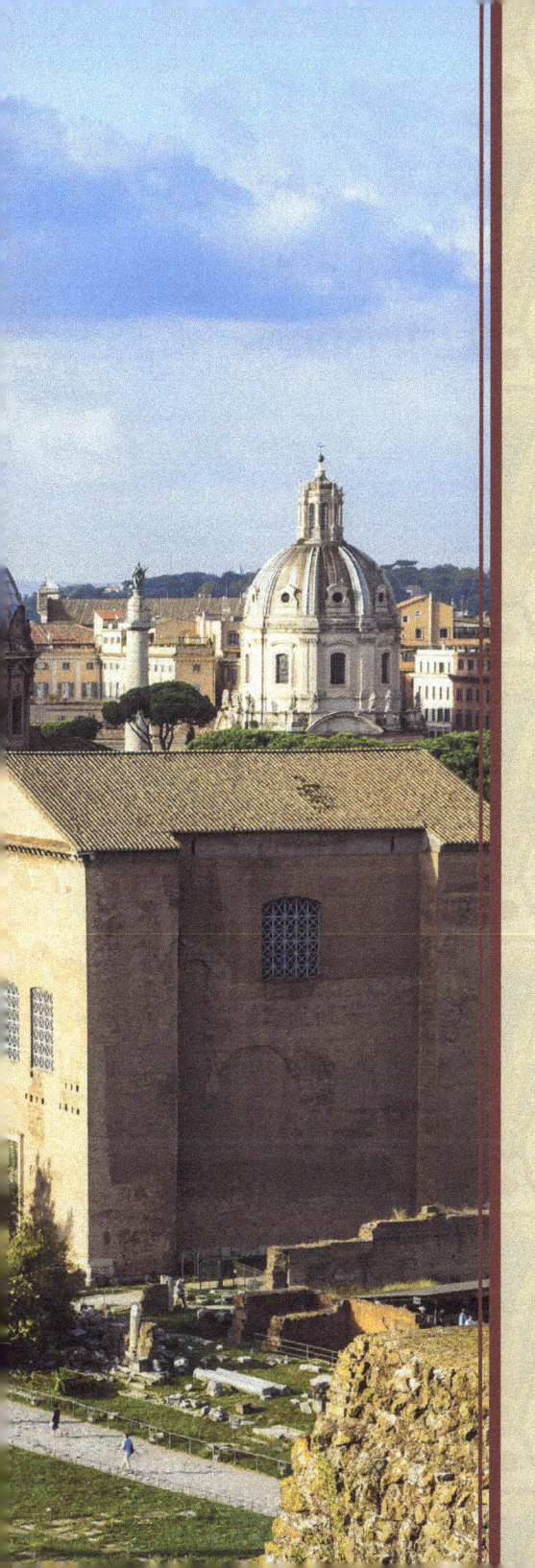

In 753 BC, Romulus went forward to build around Palatine, the hill he had selected. Remus taunted him and Romulus killed his brother. It's possible that the word "Rome" comes from the name "Romulus." Another theory is that the name "Rome" comes from the Etruscan language. The Etruscan name for the Tiber River was "Rumon."

Many different cultures blended together to become the first Romans. The Latins were the first to establish settlements in Rome.

THE SACK OF ROME ON 6 MAY 1527

**M**any Greeks came to Italy and lived along the coastline, so the Greek and Roman cultures intertwined and influenced each other.

## THE ABDUCTION OF THE SABINE WOMEN

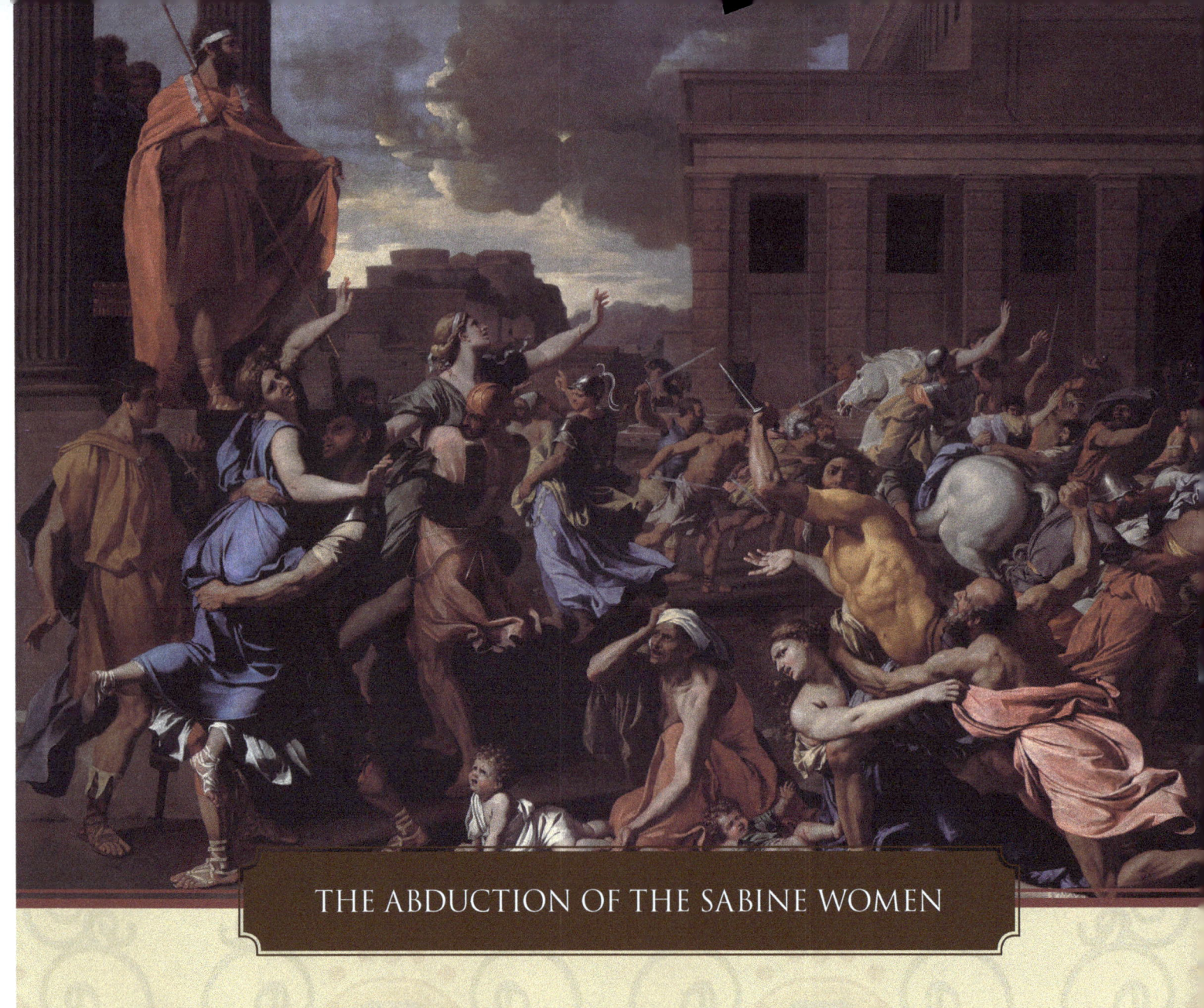

The Sabines, who lived in the Apennines Mountains, were a third group that had an impact on Roman culture.

The powerful Etruscans lived close to the city and some of them became Roman kings.

ETRUSCANS

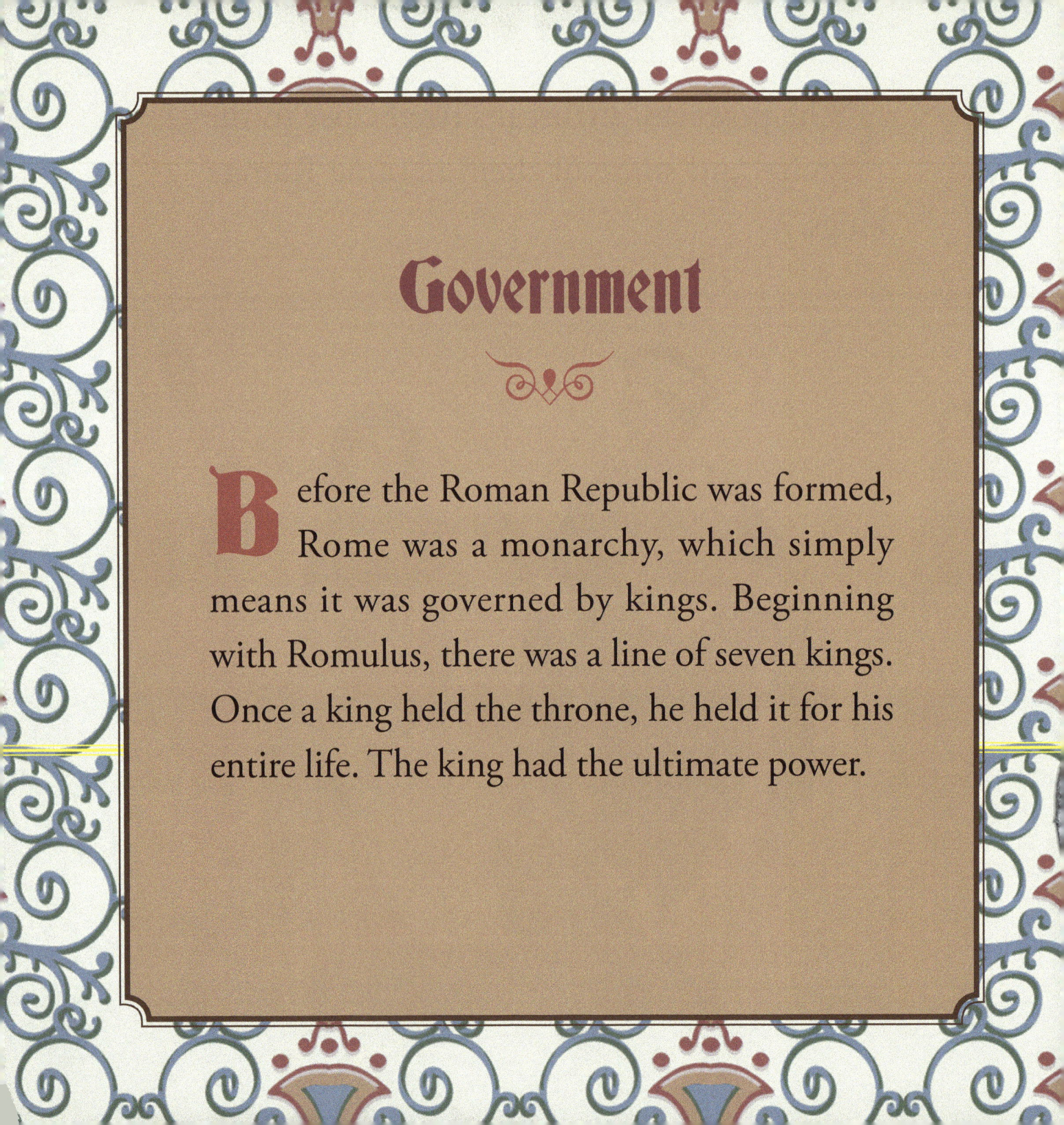

# Government

Before the Roman Republic was formed, Rome was a monarchy, which simply means it was governed by kings. Beginning with Romulus, there was a line of seven kings. Once a king held the throne, he held it for his entire life. The king had the ultimate power.

**THEODOSIUS I**
ROMAN EMPEROR FROM
AD 379 TO AD 395

CITYSCAPE OF ROME

Romulus not only acted as the head of the government, he was also the head of the Roman religion, which was a pagan religion consisting of hundreds of gods and goddesses. Even though the king was the main ruler, there were also about 300 senators who acted as the king's advisors and consultants.

TARQUINIUS

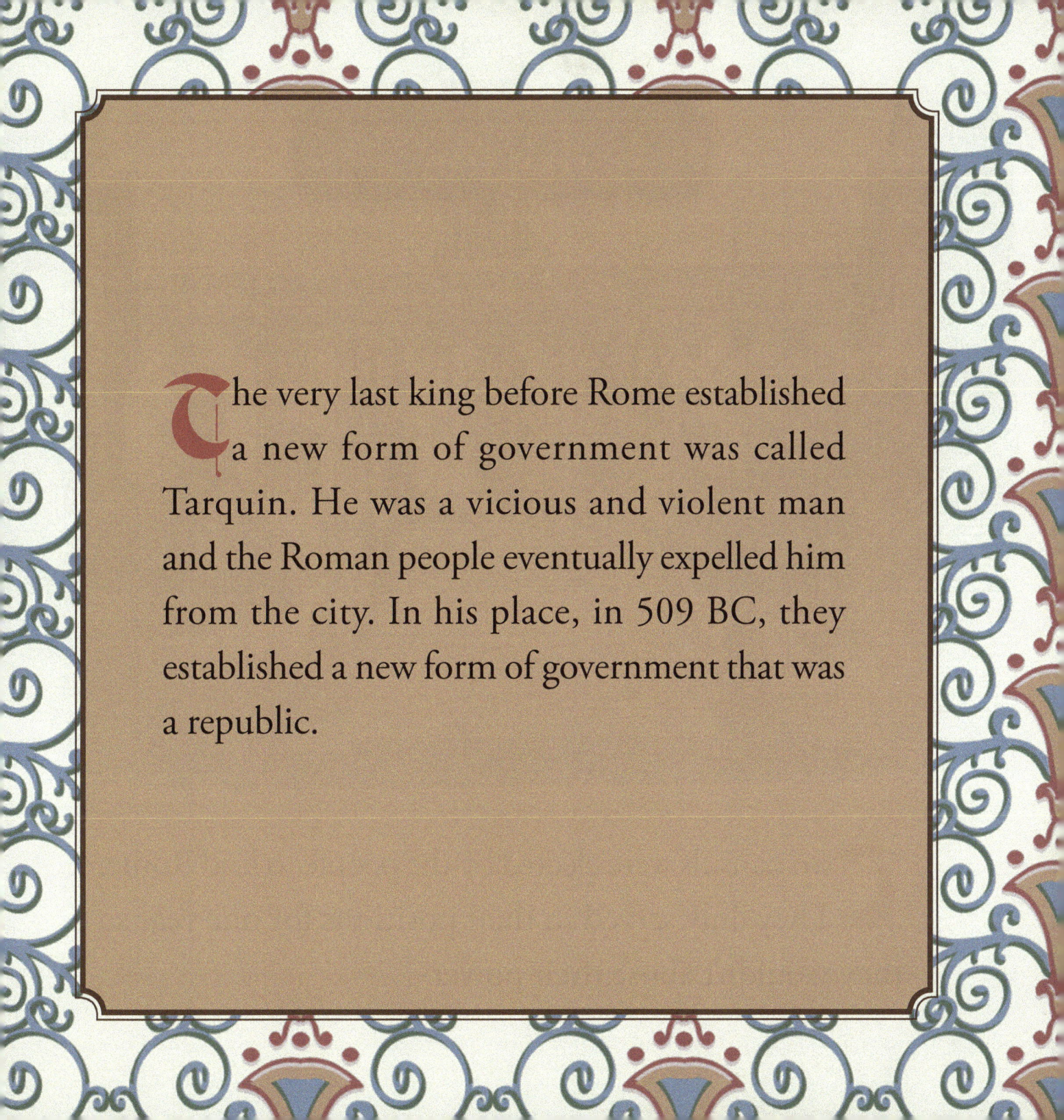

The very last king before Rome established a new form of government was called Tarquin. He was a vicious and violent man and the Roman people eventually expelled him from the city. In his place, in 509 BC, they established a new form of government that was a republic.

## CAPITOL BUILDING, ROME, ITALY

Two consuls were elected by the people to lead Rome. They only served in their positions for one year so they wouldn't abuse their power.

The senate took a more active part in governing. This form of government was successful and Rome began to become very powerful and expanded to form an empire.

## ANCIENT ROME GOVERNMENT BUILDINGS

# Science

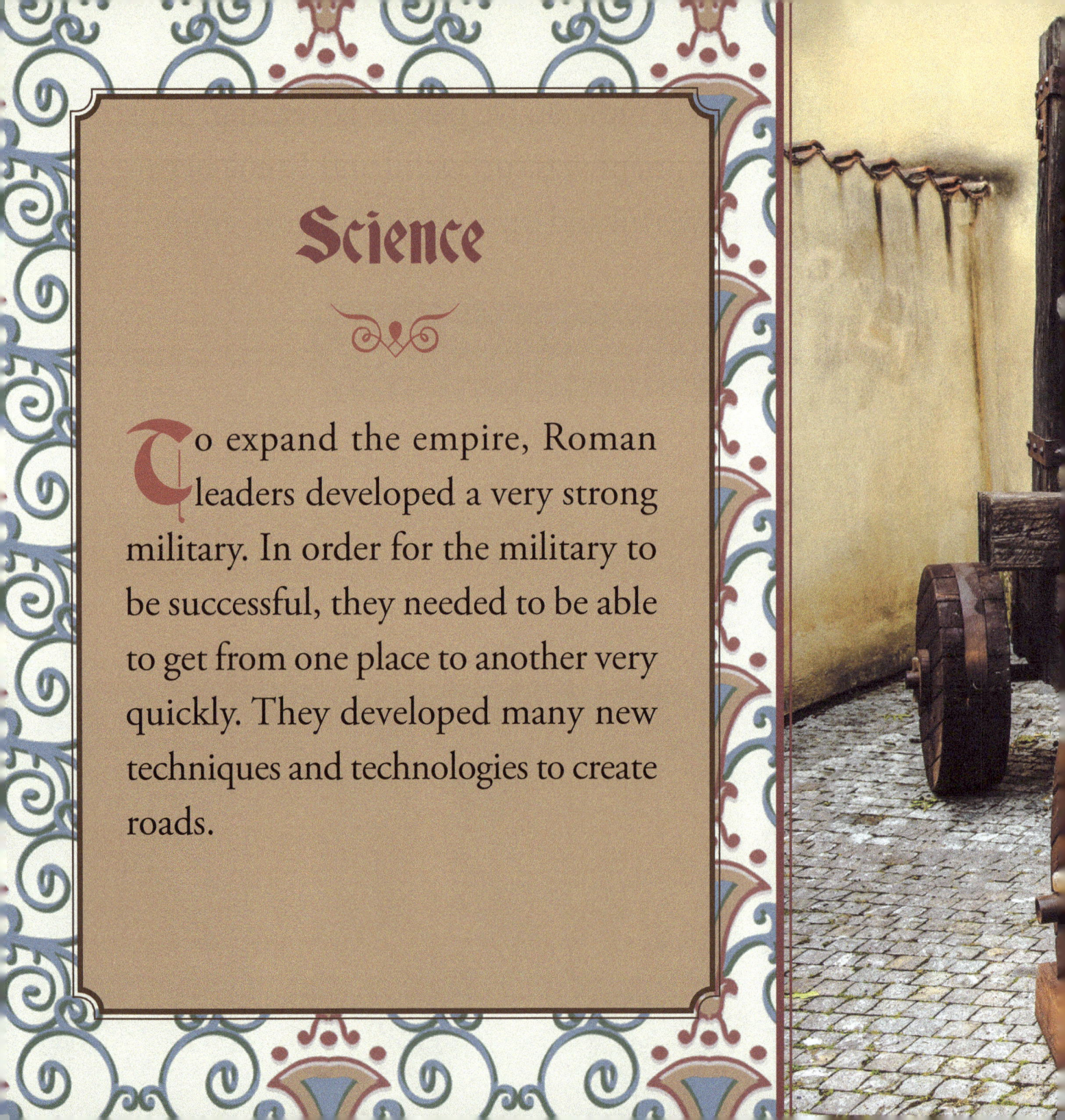

To expand the empire, Roman leaders developed a very strong military. In order for the military to be successful, they needed to be able to get from one place to another very quickly. They developed many new techniques and technologies to create roads.

## CATAPULT
### AN ANCIENT MILITARY WEAPON

ANCIENT STONE PAVEMENT IN ROME

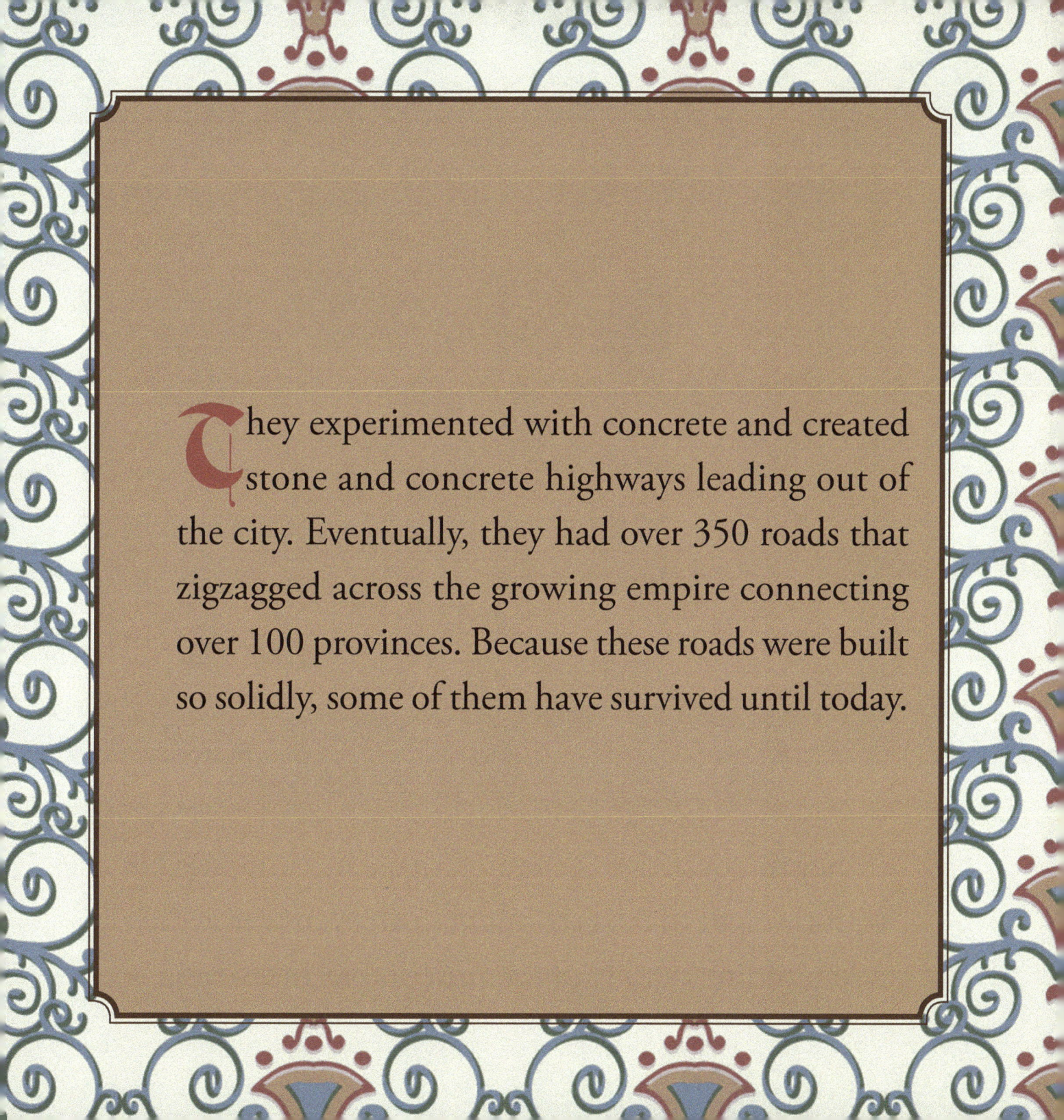

They experimented with concrete and created stone and concrete highways leading out of the city. Eventually, they had over 350 roads that zigzagged across the growing empire connecting over 100 provinces. Because these roads were built so solidly, some of them have survived until today.

## ANCIENT ROMAN RUINS

They discovered that the arch shape made it possible for weight to be distributed in an even way, which made buildings and bridges more stable and strong.

## ANCIENT ROMAN CRANE

This technology contributed to their innovations in architecture. They were avid builders and continued to create tools for faster building construction, such as cranes.

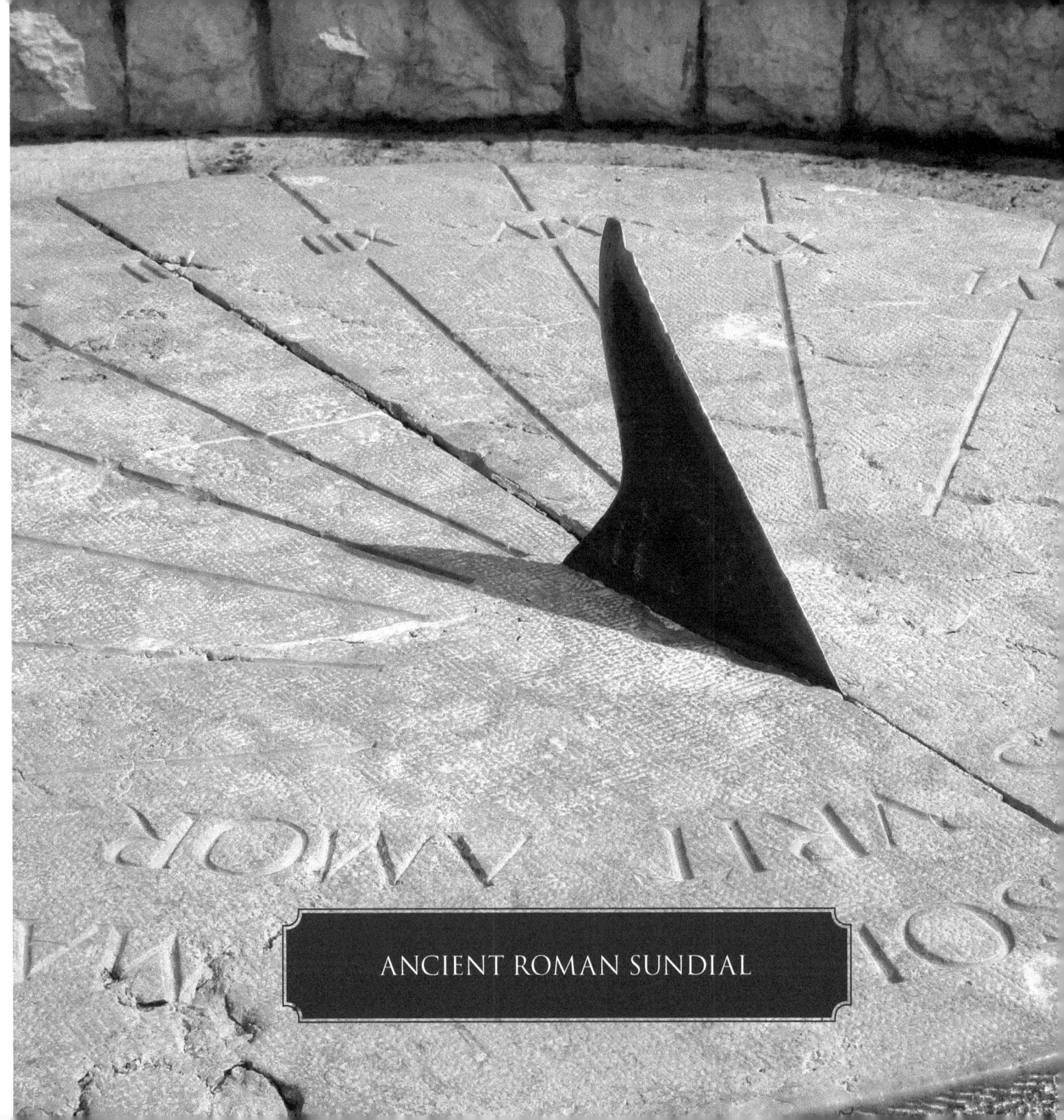

ANCIENT ROMAN SUNDIAL

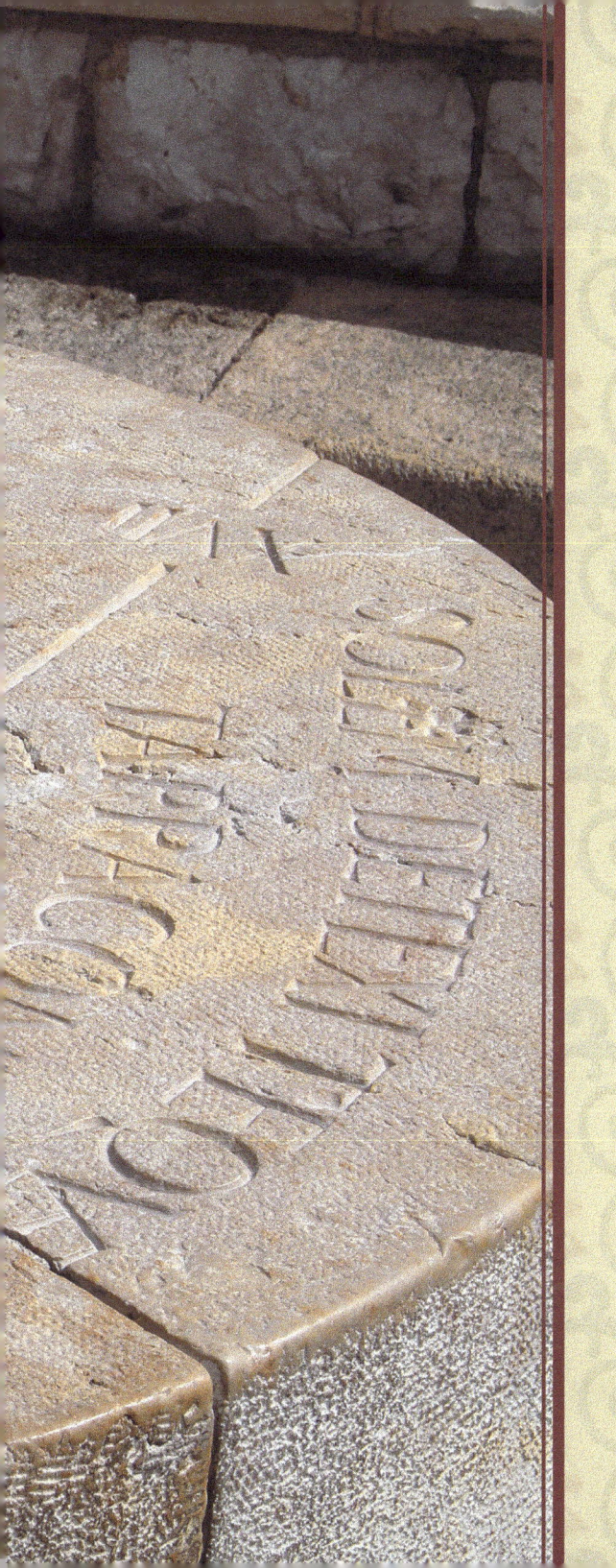

Roman citizens referred to sundials to measure time and they also created types of sundials that were portable. They had other types of measuring tools and they also had drills that were manual and spikes made of metal that were similar to modern nails.

**ANCIENT ROMAN GLASS BOWL WITH A LIGHT BLUE TINT**

The Romans had advanced techniques for blowing glass. They used this technology to create glass for windows and glass for oil lamps. Historical manuscripts note that the Romans also had mirrors.

## BODY ARMOR

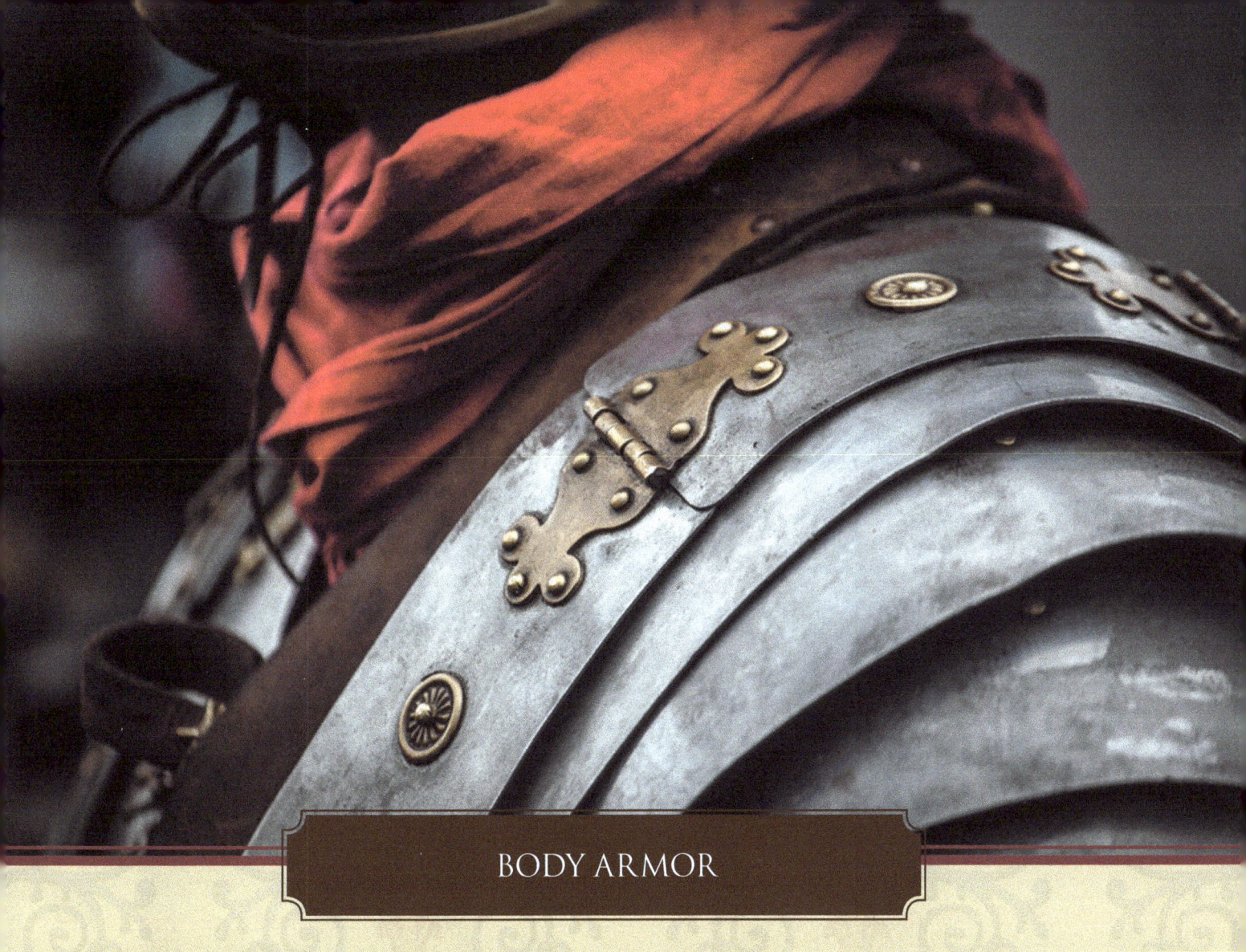

**R**efinements in weapons meant that the shields and armor that Roman soldiers used were superior to those used by other countries.

ANCIENT ROMAN WARRIORS

Their skill in the creation of weapons and roads combined with their military power allowed them to take over much of the known world as their empire expanded.

They built windmills for pulverizing corn and pumping water as well as presses designed to create olive oil from the abundant olives available in the area.

The Romans were somewhat obsessed with cleanliness. In addition to their public baths, homes for the wealthy had the luxury of indoor plumbing. Their sewers carried the human waste from indoor toilets to the Tiber River.

ANCIENT ROMAN PUBLIC BATH

# Architecture

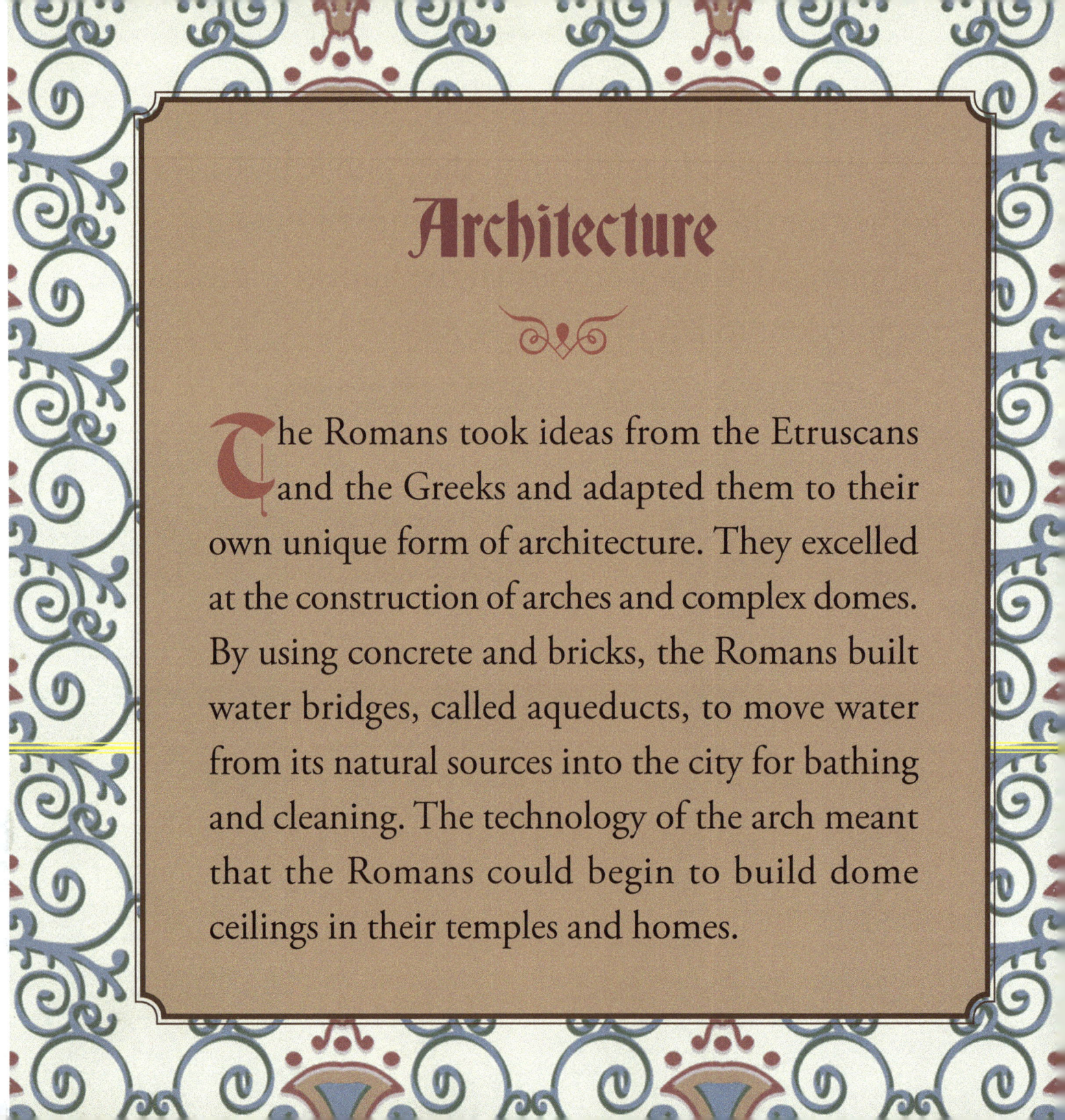

The Romans took ideas from the Etruscans and the Greeks and adapted them to their own unique form of architecture. They excelled at the construction of arches and complex domes. By using concrete and bricks, the Romans built water bridges, called aqueducts, to move water from its natural sources into the city for bathing and cleaning. The technology of the arch meant that the Romans could begin to build dome ceilings in their temples and homes.

PONT DU GARD IS AN OLD ROMAN AQUEDUCT

# THE COLOSSEUM

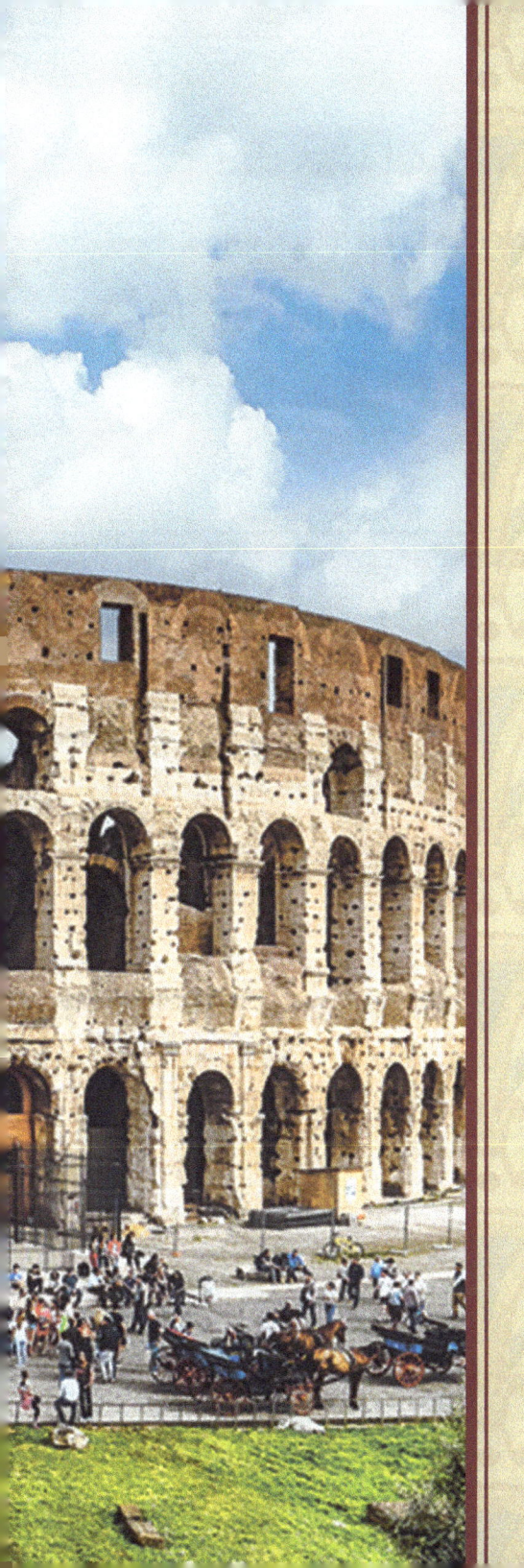

They used bricks that they created and marble from quarries to construct many of their structures. Roman amphitheaters were built throughout the empire. These amazing outdoor theaters with several levels of seating were used to present chariot races as well as bloody gladiator fights and executions. Over 200 amphitheaters were built throughout the empire and many of them have pieces that are still standing. The Colosseum is a famous example of one of these enormous oval structures.

Another famous architectural marvel was the Roman Forum, which was constructed of stone in a large rectangular shape. This building was used for elections and speeches as well as for trials.

ROMAN FORUM

A common public structure was the Thermae, which was essentially a bathhouse. The Romans used these public baths not only as a place to cleanse themselves but also to socialize and gossip.

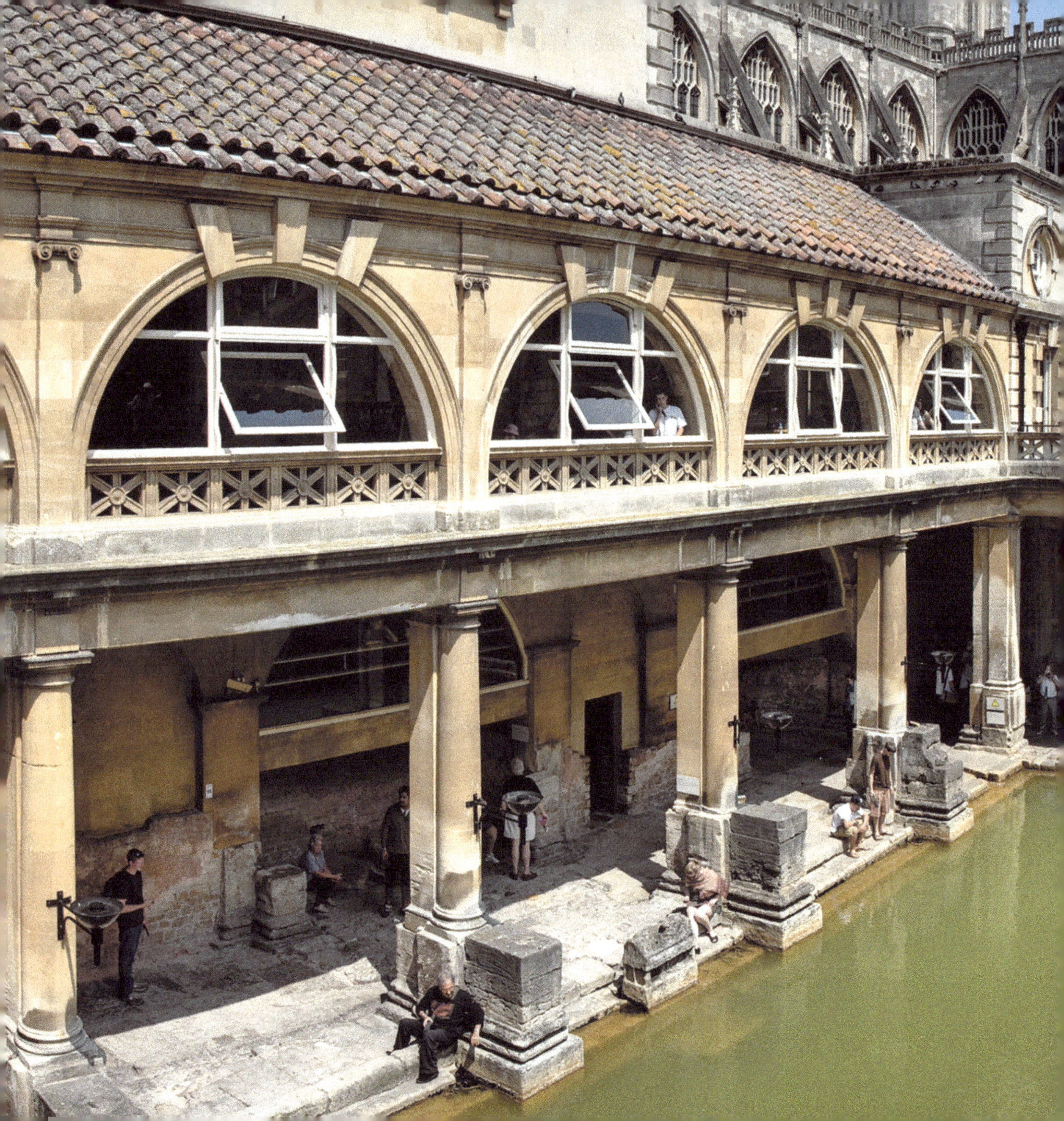

Baths were offered at various temperatures--cold, warm, and hot. The Thermae also had beautiful gardens and an open area called an atrium where the citizens could rest and reflect. Some used the atrium to exercise, stretch, or wrestle.

Not all the buildings in Rome were for public use. Some were private residences for the wealthy with elaborate carvings created in the walls of stone.

These homes frequently had atriums to soak up the warmth of the sun. Walls and floors featured beautiful arrangements of stone and glass in mosaics.

# PAINTINGS AND SCULPTURES OF ANCIENT ROME

# Art

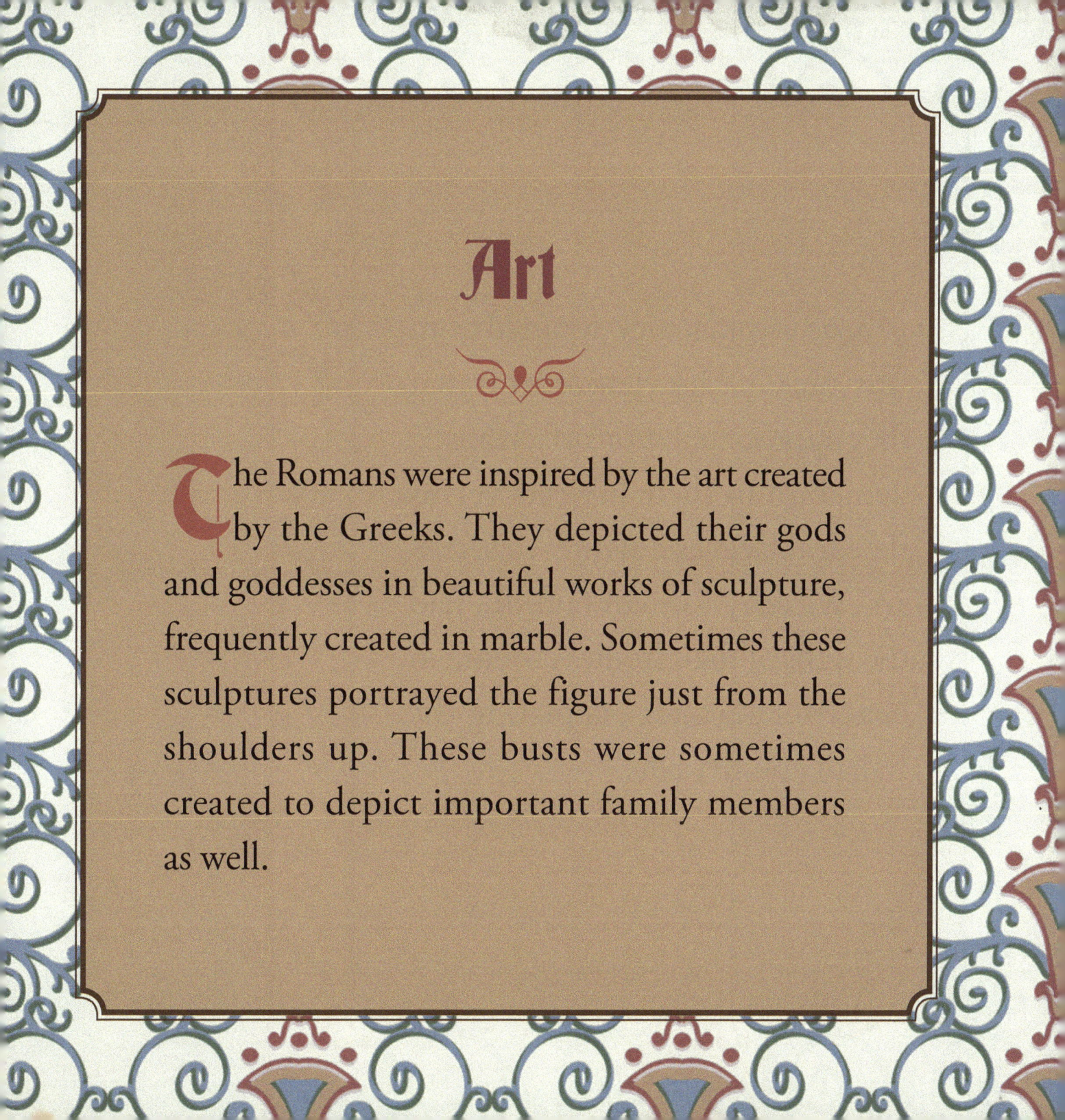

The Romans were inspired by the art created by the Greeks. They depicted their gods and goddesses in beautiful works of sculpture, frequently created in marble. Sometimes these sculptures portrayed the figure just from the shoulders up. These busts were sometimes created to depict important family members as well.

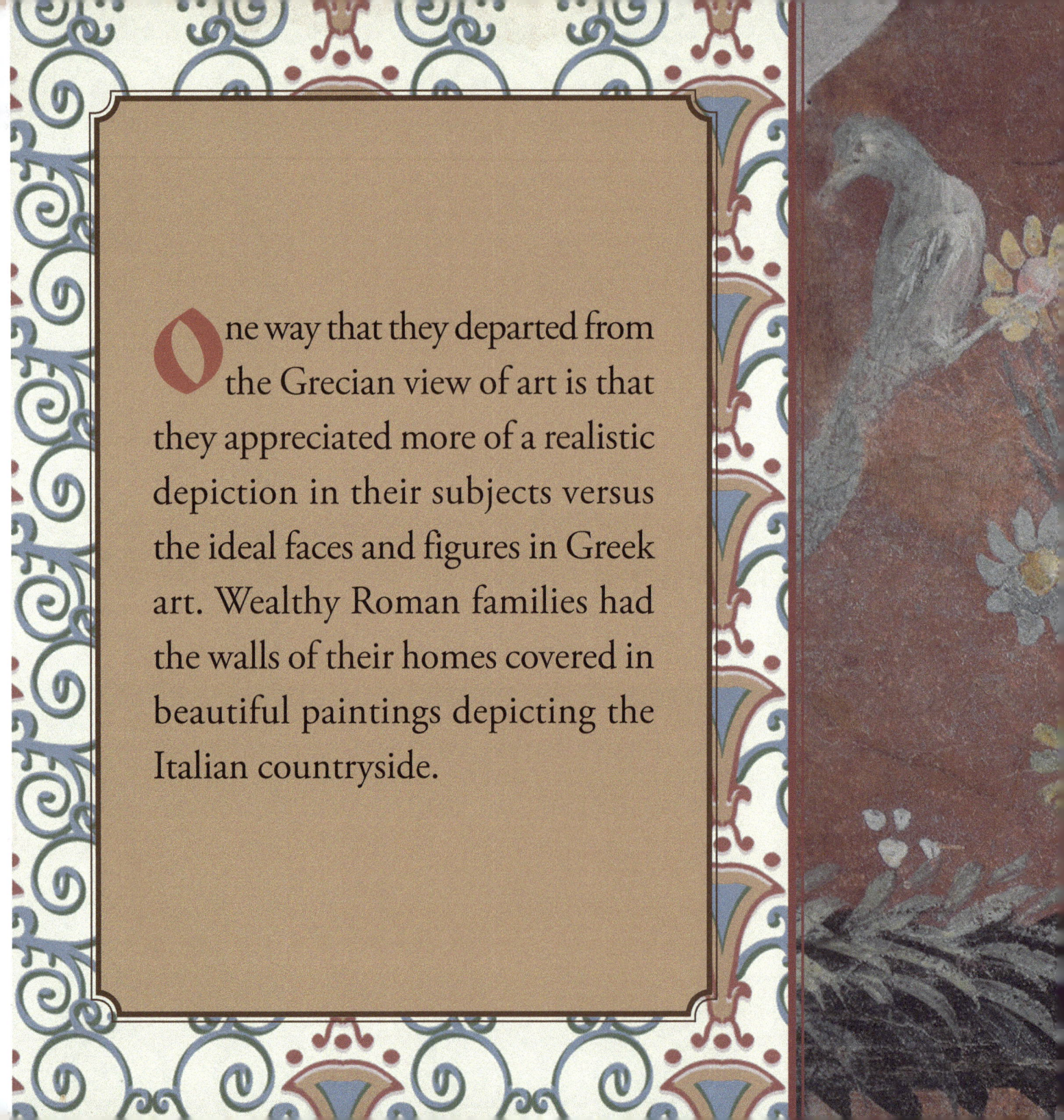

One way that they departed from the Grecian view of art is that they appreciated more of a realistic depiction in their subjects versus the ideal faces and figures in Greek art. Wealthy Roman families had the walls of their homes covered in beautiful paintings depicting the Italian countryside.

WALL PAINTING FRAGMENT WITH FLOWERS AND A BIRD, FROM A ROMAN VILLA

# ITALIAN COUNTRYSIDE

# Summary

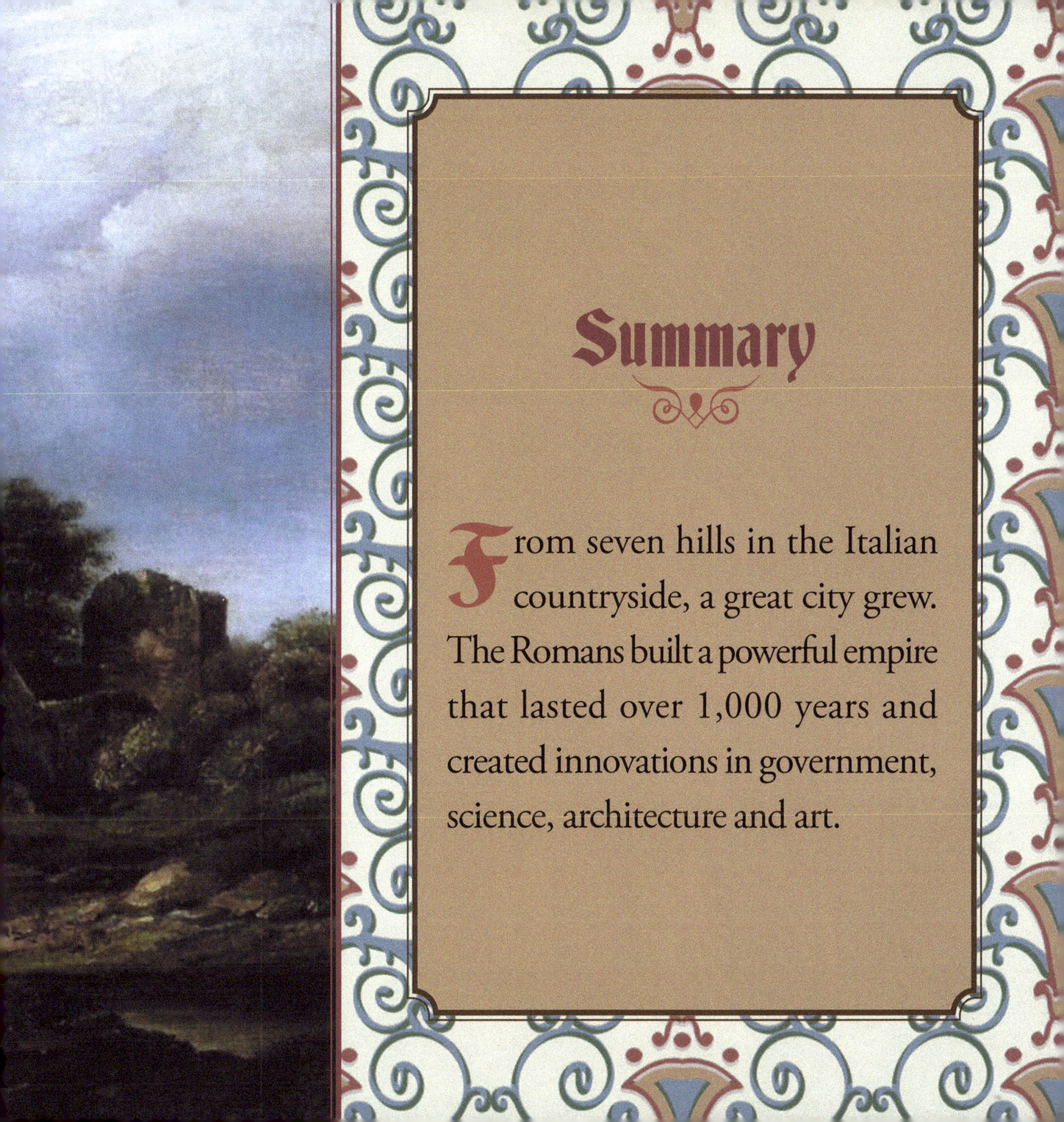

From seven hills in the Italian countryside, a great city grew. The Romans built a powerful empire that lasted over 1,000 years and created innovations in government, science, architecture and art.

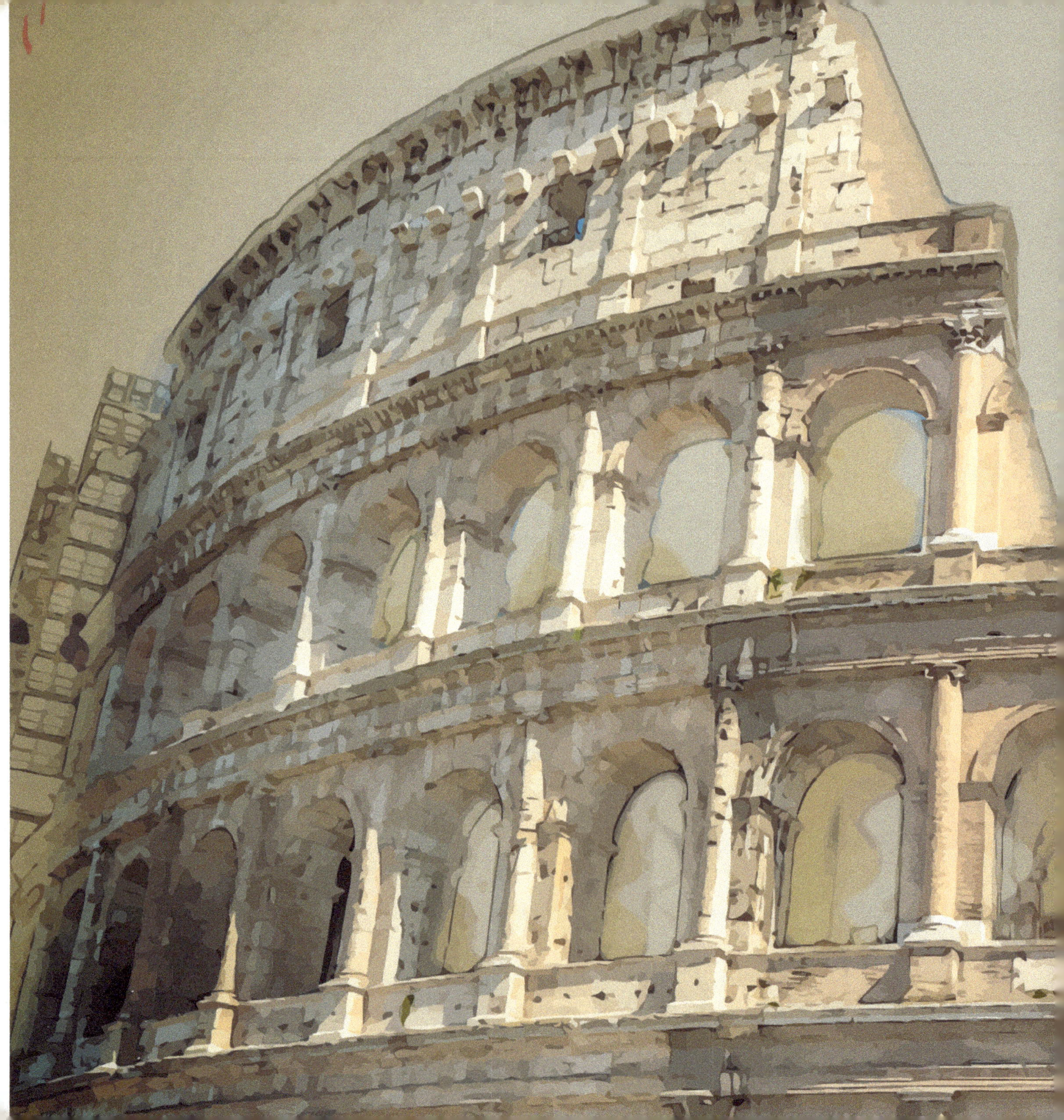

Now that you've read about the city of Rome in ancient times, you may want to read more about the architecture of Rome in the Baby Professor book *Engineering and Construction That We Can Still See Today - Ancient History Rome | Children's Ancient History.*

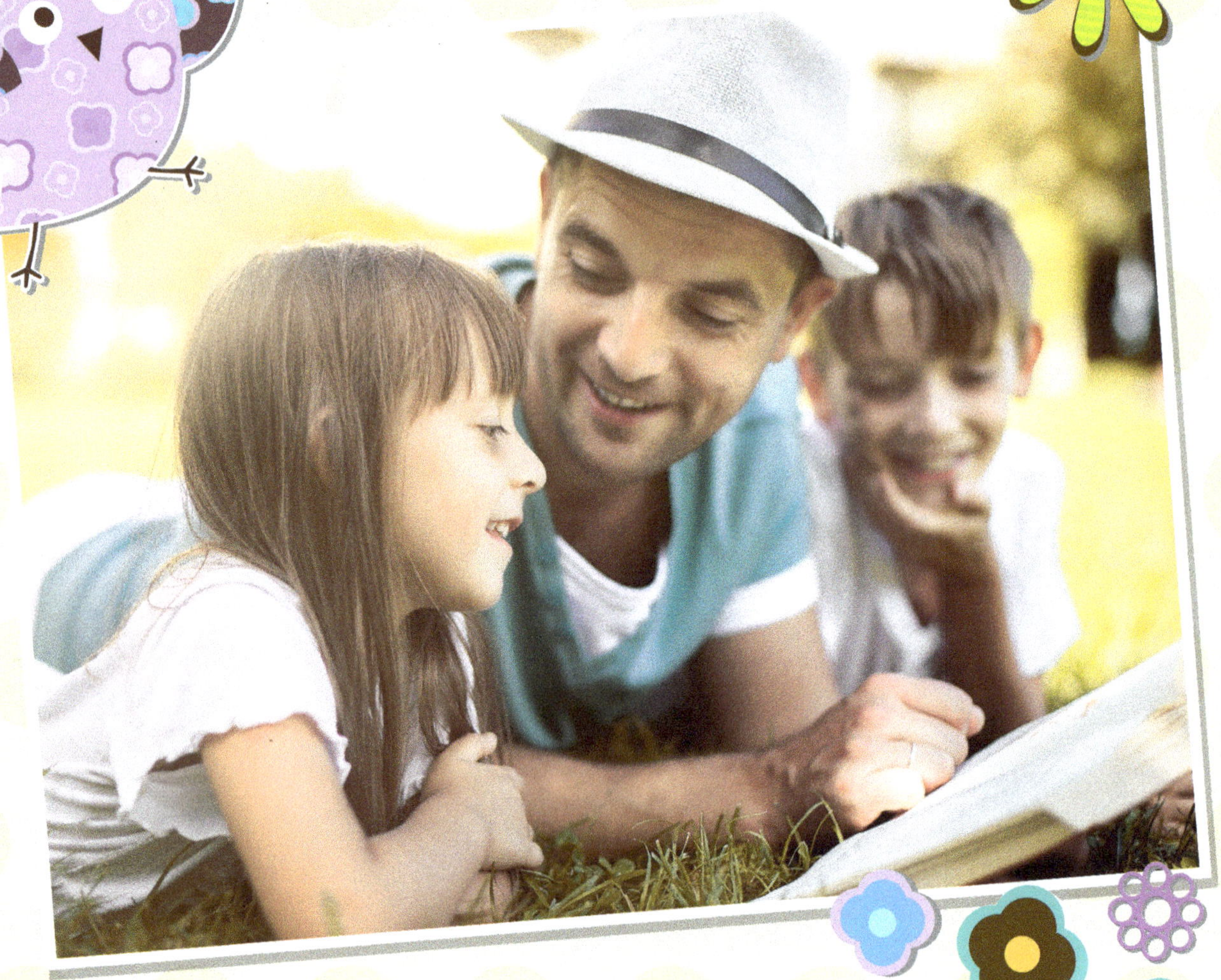

Visit

**BABY PROFESSOR**
EDUCATION KIDS

# www.BabyProfessorBooks.com

to download Free Baby Professor eBooks and view our catalog of new and exciting Children's Books